THE BALLERINA'S
LITTLE BLACK BOOK

1ST EDITION

by Brittani Marie

Copyright © 2016 Brittani Marie

All rights reserved. No parts of this publication may be
reproduced in any form, stored in a
retrieval system, or transmitted in any form whatsoever or by any means – for example,
electronic, mechanical, photocopy, recording or otherwise – without the prior written
permission of the publisher.

For information regarding bulk purchases, please contact Brown Girls Do Ballet® at
www.browngirlsdoballet.com.
Manufactured in the United States.

ISBN: 978-0-692-68115-2 (paperback)

EDITOR
Brittani Marie

EDITING ASSISTANT
Rainseford Stauffer

GRAPHIC DESIGNER
Vanessa Arty

RESEARCH ASSISTANT
Sekani Robinson

AUDITION COORDINATOR
Sherese Parris

PHOTOGRAPHERS
Arschana Images
Jasmine Alston

FEATURED DANCERS
Aesha Ash
Olivia Boisson
Misty Copeland
Tunai Denise
Jimena Flores

EDITORIAL

Jasmine Anderson
Jordyn Buehner
Andrew Eccles
Gregg Delman
Island Boi Photography
Rachel Neville
Philadelphia Dance Project
Justin Reid
Aaron Sans Madrid
Renee Scott
Pickled Thoughts
TaKiyah Wallace

Alicia Graf Mack
Sydney Magruder
Ashley Murphy
Ingrid Silva
Alison Stroming
Eliana Vaha'l Fe'ao

COVER LOOK

PHOTOGRAPHER
Jasmine Alston

CREATIVE DIRECTOR I FASHION STYLIST
Saniyyah Bilal

MODEL BALLERINA
Tunai Denise

HAIR STYLIST
Michelle Nichole

MAKE-UP ARTIST
Gogo Leopard

FASHION DESIGNER
Lillie Designs Headpiece

DESIGNER
Plain Elain

Foreword

In fall 2012, my three-year-old daughter sat in front of a television program one evening and declared she wanted to be a ballerina. Brown skin, thick afro, tiny body, amazed and completely enamored by a graceful white swan. Of course she wanted to be a ballerina--Don't all little girls go through that? As a mom, I was sure this was the first of many wishes she would have over the course of her life. Some would be realistic, some far-fetched, and yet, I knew I had to do my best to attempt to make this dream happen.

Founder, TaKiyah Wallace and Daughter Charlie Reese | Photo Credit: ©Omar Ramos

In 2012, when she made this declaration, my only knowledge of ballet extended to a production of Coppélia I had attended in college. I had no clue how or where to find a class, or what it might eventually take to get my daughter on stage just like the swan she saw on television. So I did what most people do: I Googled. I searched for days, looking for information and local studios near me. After visiting countless sites, I realized very quickly that you don't see very many "brown girls" in ballet. Pick up any dance magazine, or better yet, go to a major ballet production and count them. They are a rarity. As a photographer, I knew first-hand the power of images, could change this under representation by by photographing ballerinas of color and displaying them on my very small social media channels. This is what sparked the beginning of the Brown Girls Do Ballet® organization.

A few months later, in 2013, I met a vibrant young lady who was immensely passionate about this mission. Brittani spent nearly her entire life as a brown ballerina, but despite being incredibly talented, she decided not to pursue a professional career. In the early stages of Brown Girls Do Ballet, her educational background in public relations combined with her expertise in marketing proved to be a tremendous asset in ensuring we sent the right message to aspiring dancers. Artistically, she was helpful inselecting images which honored the classical technique standards to display on our platform. She wouldn't hesitate to pester me if she saw a sickled foot or bad turnout. I love her for it now, as her foresight gave this burgeoning organization credibility. We spent hours, days at a time, researching, interviewing and meeting different ballerinas to understand what they really needed. It was during these very long hours that light bulb switched on.

When Brittani first pitched the idea for a guide specifically written for brown ballerinas, I immediately saw the big picture: A book created just for ballerinas of color. It was a long shot, but a necessary one. Originally, it was supposed to be a calendar with a small resource guide in the back. So, we cast twelve dancers from the New York tri-state area and recruited up and coming dance photographer Justin Reid for a full twelve-hour photo session. We kicked off the shoot at the crack of dawn with dancer Chelsea Simone leaping across Fifth Avenue, and busy New Yorkers helping us interrupt traffic. (page 48) It was nothing short of an amazing adventure. Once we saw the photos, Brittani realized we had to give young girls more than just a calendar.

"They've waited too long for just photos... we have to give them more than that. They need to actually hear from prominent ballerinas they can relate to."

Fast forward about eight months: The already chaotic idea of interviewing high-profile dancers and publishing a book reached new levels of chaos when Brittani landed her dream media job in NYC and my very own brown ballerina became a big sister.

Although life tried to intervene, our love for Brown Girls Do Ballet triumphed. Brittani called me and accepted her calling to be a Co-Founder. Nearly one year later, The Ballerina's Little Black Book was finally born.

We came to realize the impact of representation, or lack thereof, was much bigger than ballet itself. It was about being a woman of color and having role models to grant vision. Permission to dream. The Ballerina's Little Black Book is a much-needed tool that will hopefully give a profound sense of self-worth to dancers of color throughout their training. It highlights the connection between academics and performing arts. It introduces you to some of the trailblazers that have paved the way and the dancers currently on the front lines. For the little brown girls who watch television shows and dream of being just like the graceful swan, The Ballerina's Little Black Book makes their dream real and attainable. My hope is that young girls who never thought ballet was possible for them, may see reflections of themselves in this book. This book is for little girls like my daughter who, although she may be little and her skin may be brown, of course...she is fierce.

With love and dancing full out,

TaKiyah Wallace

TaKiyah Wallace-McMillian
Founder, Brown Girls Do Ballet

MAHOGANY BLUES

DANCE APPAREL

NUDE DANCEWEAR WITH
EVERY SHADE IN MIND

MBDANCEAPPAREL.COM

CONTENTS

14
CHAPTER 1
ENDLESS POSSIBILITIES:
A look into the life of a ballerina
AESHA ASH

19
CHAPTER 2
BEGINNING BALLET
A mini guide for brown ballerinas

26
CHAPTER 3
ALISON STROMING'S DANCE BAG ESSENTIALS
Being prepared for the road ahead
ALISON STROMING

34
FROM BARRE TO POINTE:
A brand that understands diversity
GAYNOR MINDEN

38
CHAPTER 4
AUDITION TIPS
How she made it into the ranks of New York City Ballet
OLIVIA BOISSON

44
CHAPTER 5
POWER IN AUTHENTICITY
The extraordinary is possible when you embrace your true self
INGRID SILVA

48
CHAPTER 6
THE RECIPE FOR A HEALTHY BODY IMAGE
Avoiding unhealthy comparisons
SYDNEY MAGRUDER

54
CHAPTER 7
JOURNEY THROUGH ANGUISHED PASSION FEATURE STORY
TUNAI DENISE

60
CHAPTER 8
BEYOND THE BARRE:
Dance Education
ALICIA GRAF MACK

65
CHAPTER 9
A MESSAGE TO BROWN BALLERINAS
MISTY COPELAND

69
TRAINING & SCHOLARSHIPS

72
THANK YOU & ACKNOLEWDGMENTS

Dancer: Sydney Winston | ©TaKiyah Wallace, Brown Girls Do Ballet

The highest potential...

Once again, I found myself staring at my last pair of pointe shoes. Sounds of Tchaikovsky's Sugar Plum Fairy filled my imagination. My satin, blush-pink ribbons now rest, un-dyed...I am reminded of my first love. Extravagant costumes for spring recitals, summers spent away dancing, and friends from around the world. I didn't have a simple childhood like many of my peers. I had a worldly one. Then, my thoughts are interrupted by the inevitable nagging question- Why on earth did I stop dancing? Was it a lack of courage that altered my prima ballerina dreams? Perhaps feelings of isolation or insecurity convinced me ballet was a fantasy world. But I can't help but wonder what a difference it would have made to know Ingrid Silva was growing up in Brazil, dancing her heart out to venture to America. Aesha Ash was teaching herself Italian, as she toured across Europe. To know there were women like me, who shared my vision and made it happen from humble beginnings.

To this day, the benefits gained from being immersed in a refined European art do not go unnoticed. Presence. Tenacity. Courage. Yet, I am sometimes confronted with a regret of not reaching my fullest potential. Oh, the places I could have seen, the connections I could have made. As Aesha shares, experiences are what allow for a deeper understanding of our differences. I couldn't agree with her more.

To be a ballerina of color is an overwhelming experience of cultural exchange and determination. With that being said, the first edition of The Ballerina's Little Black Book highlights resilience and purpose. It encourages individuality in the face of adversity. We hope the words of these empowered women can demonstrate the rewards of going against the odds regardless of what life has in store for you. As we go further into this great world, dreams may change. Not every little girl will want to become a professional ballerina. That's completely okay, but let this be proof that ballet training is a disciplined activity that can set the foundation for many chapters to come. Remember, in whatever you pursue, to seek your highest potential for achievement. Dance your way through life.

With Love and Admiration,

Brittani Marie

Brittani Marie
Co-Founder
Brown Girls Do Ballet®

Editor's Note

Dancer: Aesha Ash
Photo Credit: ©Renee Scott

ENDLESS POSSIBILITIES

A Look Into the Life of a Ballerina

Aesha Ash

A *long-time inspiration because of her defiance of stereotypes and exceptional grace, at the tender age of 18, her career journeyed from the prestigious corps of New York City Ballet, to film appearances and a international soloist position in Europe. For nearly eight years, she was challenged by being the only black ballerina in her company, a position in which she was enormously successful despite lacking professional mentors in the industry. Aesha overcame doubts and many insecurities to discover her real purpose. With grace and soft-spoken eloquence, the current mother of two embodies the many benefits of becoming a ballerina.*

I am from inner city Rochester, NY- proudly so. I was raised in a working-class family and had to fight a lot to overcome many stereotypes attached to African American communities.

Initially, I was not very interested in ballet. I began dancing at the age of 5 but my childhood dream was to become an archeologist. My goals in taking ballet were to improve my technique in the other forms of dance I was studying at the time (jazz and tap). Since they came much easier to me, I soon became bored with them and changed course to explore the challenges of ballet.

I was not a "born ballerina" and had to work extremely hard at it. Early in my training, there came a point where I began to understand how difficult it would be to become a ballerina, as a woman of color. I liked the idea of taking on that challenge. Since my childhood, I have always had the desire to dispel stereotypes that surround African-Americans.

By age 13, I was accepted to the School of American Ballet (SAB), the official school of New York City Ballet. I had no ballet or professional mentors to guide me on my journey. I relied heavily on family, faith, and friends for confidence. They were vital to me making it through each and every day.

My hard work began to be noticed, and I received the Mae L. Wien Award for Outstanding Promise during my last year of training. I became a corps member of City Ballet by the time I was 18.

I remained with City Ballet for eight years before moving to Europe. I joined Béjart Ballet in Lausanne, Switzerland as a soloist. While I was successful, I began to experience feelings of being isolated. In 2005, I moved to San Francisco 2005 and became a member of Alonzo King's Lines Ballet. It was

"If we could clear our minds of all the images we have been exposed to that led us to believing we are not worthy, we would soon realize that our differences are not handicaps."

there that I found a revival of my love for dancing. I am truly honored that my ballet career also led to so many other opportunities. I've been featured in the New York Times, Dance Magazine and among others. Dancing as a stunt double for Zoe Saldana in the film Center Stage was very intimidating for me. I was never a big fan of watching videos of myself and was petrified by the idea of being captured for a movie that would repeatedly be shown. Looking back, I wish I could have been less insecure and enjoyed the entire experience much more. Still, I feel very lucky I had the opportunity to dance a role in such an important film for dancers.

Having pursued an international career, I have come to believe every experience in life shapes who we are. Travel, for example, enriches our lives and connects us as human beings. It exposed me to culture in ways I would never have experienced staying at home. It enriched my artistry as well. Working with dancers from various backgrounds, styles and teachings was an eye-opening experience and one I believe all dancers or young girls should hope to have. I taught myself French and have since learned Italian (while sadly losing most of my French), and have been pushed outside of my comfort zone on many occasions. Now, I feel very at home outside my country. I have an even greater love of other cultures. All of this would not have been possible if it were not for the travel I had done as a dancer. Through language, culture, and so many opportunities to delve into the depths of new cultures, ballet soon became a perfect vehicle for me to spread the message I seemed always to hold: That we are more than a stereotype.

There are enormous benefits to studying ballet as an art form. Those benefits should not be limited to one particular race or socio-economic group. Diverse environments also enhance our lives and help us understand and connect with one another. Seeing the ballet world embrace more diverse images of beauty not only builds the self-esteem of so many young women and girls with, but stands as an example to the world that socio-economic status does not define beauty, talent or grace.

I encountered many moments of doubt and insecurity being a brown ballerina from an inner city. Nevertheless, as with each experience, I learned and grew a great deal from it. There is no need to waste your energy on negative self-talk: it will become a habit that is almost impossible to break. No individual can put limitations on you unless you give them the power to.

To aspiring ballerinas: Focus on knowing your craft inside and out. Don't waste time wondering what others think of you. I only began understanding my work upon retiring. It is so important to know the work you are doing. Otherwise, you may waste a lot of time and energy trying to perfect something you know little about. Research the various styles of ballet, their origins or notable dancers who were exceptional performers. You now have the luxury of learning valuable tips from sources such as youtube videos. Finding the right mentor can also provide a tremendous amount of support. Although I did not have one, I could have benefited tremendously from having one during my career.

To connect with Aesha and learn more about what she's up to, check out her organization, Swan Dreams Project, which aims to spread positive images of women of color. She will be happy to hear from you!

www.swandreamsproject.com

Ashley Murphy
Washington Ballet

"Ballet is life-changing whether you become a professional or not. It teaches us to respect our bodies and the world around us. From a young age I learned the importance of hard work, dedication, and time management. I owe that to my classical training."

Photo Credit: ©Rachel Neville 2015

Ch.2

BEGINNING BALLET

A Mini Guide for Brown Ballerinas

If you once dreamed of wearing a romantic tutu (or seeing your daughter in one), you are not alone. Over the past few years, women of various backgrounds from all over the world have shared their childhood dreams of being a ballerina with us. While one of the most significant questions surrounding ballet is the lack of diversity, it seems there is also a lack of guidance for a larger audience, too.

Recognizing different demographics have different needs, in all of life's disciplines, would benefit us all. I believe, opportunities are made possible through increased understanding of expectations and how to navigate roadblocks. It is true that ballet is generally expensive, time consuming, and recommended to start early (ideally between the ages of four to eight.) Ballet is challenging enough on its own, so to break down barriers and deepen the conversation, we've put together a mini beginners guide based on the many challenges of brown ballerinas.

THINKING OUTSIDE THE BOX

WHY BALLET

Before we dive into how to start, for the main purpose of this book, I'd like to confirm why it's important: The benefits. First, it should be noted that participation in performing arts has a tremendous positive impact on academic performance. If you're already dancing your heart out after school, here are even more reasons to be super proud of your stellar ballet skills:

• Studies on Greenville Ballet School's website, indicate students involved in the arts are four times more likely to be recognized for academic achievement. Running for class office? You're three times more likely to be elected.
• High school students who participate in the arts have higher math and verbal SAT scores.
• If your parents aren't rich, being involved in the arts still means that you're more than twice as likely to graduate college than your peers.

One study even found higher GPAs among students who were dancers. Perhaps this is explains why countries with the highest ranking math and science scores make arts and music education programs mandatory (Japan, Hungary, and Netherlands.)

But that relationship is not just found between academics and arts. I will be the first to attest that involvement in the arts creates a social awareness that encourages persistence and responsibility. You also have less time for watching television and are generally more excited about learning. Ambition ignites a natural curiosity. Even if you decide not to be a professional ballerina, did you know that 72% of business leaders say creativity is the number-one characteristic they look for? I've yet to have one job interview that overlooked "ballerina" in the activities section of my resume. It says something about you. To put it simply, ballet matters, and being a ballet dancer matters. You will soon understand why ballerinas are so passionate about their foundation.

FINDING A STUDIO

Depending on where you live, there can be a variety of classes to choose from. But that isn't the issue. Finding an affordable studio where there's at least another brown friendly face is. The harsh truth: unless you're in a huge metropolitan city like New York or LA, there will likely be very few mini-fro rocking ballerinas like you see on social media. They're scattered. However this doesn't mean dismiss the journey. Our advice? Approach the task of finding a dance studio just as you approach finding the right school.

- **SEASONS:** Dance classes typically follow the academic calendar (starting in Fall or Winter, with select summer programs). If interested, begin your research before school starts.

- **WORD OF MOUTH:** Ask other parents or peers who take dance classes about their studios. The cost will vary depending on what they are enrolled in, their location, and class level, which means you should do follow up research before making a decision.

- **RESEARCH:** In addition to scanning the websites of local ballet companies, check your academic school's website to see if there is a current or future program in the works. School art programs are usually more cost effective, if not free. They can also give students a preview of ballet without a huge commitment.

- **CLASS VISITS:** Don't rely on social media or the website to accurately show how diverse a studio is. Set up an appointment to view a class and speak with the instructor. When visiting, keep in mind that ballet derived from a classical European culture. The nature of the discipline may not appear warm and inviting at first (I was once put out of class for laughing too much!). This doesn't mean studio owners don't want diversity. Keep an open mind and initiate a relationship with them. Get any questions answered. As mentioned earlier, ballet can be expensive, so you will want to get estimates of all the costs related to costumes, recitals, and other expenses early on. Feel free to let them know your reservations. This is how we begin to diversify ballet!

ATTIRE

As a disclaimer, please be aware that every studio has different rules and it's not unusual for them to include a dress code or hair requirements. The idea is to concentrate on understanding your body and remove distractions. Generally speaking, ballet classes will require you to wear a leotard, pink or flesh tone tights, with ballet shoes. Jewelry is usually not allowed for safety reasons. Hair is to be placed neatly in a bun and out of the face. Nude dance apparel will be needed for recitals to wear under costumes. To get an idea of prices, I recommend requesting a catalog from Discount Dance Supply. If there is a dance apparel store in your hometown, it's always great to pay them a visit and consult on the appropriate items needed in the long run. We will get into items to carry in your dance bag with Alison Stroming in Chapter 4.

RECITALS

Recitals and performances are a very exciting time of year for dancers! You finally get to show off all the hard work you've

Dancer: Sydney Winston | ©TaKiyah Wallace, Brown Girls Do Ballet

done throughout the year. Dance studios typically have one to two recitals or performances per year (following the Fall and Spring seasons). Dancers and parents should expect to have extended rehearsals as early as a month out leading up to show time. If new shoes are needed, be sure to purchase them at least a month in advance so they are comfortable for recital night. Please be informed this is also the period where you will begin to spend many late nights and weekends in rehearsals (hence why there's less time for TV). This can be grueling at times, but is also where you learn the true importance of being prepared and managing time wisely. I recall many late nights completing homework backstage- it was challenging and incredible all at once. Getting rest while you can will make all the difference.

ADVANCED TRAINING

As you get further into ballet training, it is important to explore the various methods taught outside your home studio (such as Vaganova or Cecchetti) to have a better understanding of the various techniques. Being familiar with the different methods is crucial when auditioning, as different companies adhere to different methods. Throughout the school year, studios shift their focus to performance preparation, so it is the student's responsibility to keep their technique strong, and use the things they've worked on in class all semester onstage. This is where summer intensive trainings come into play, and they will probably be the most memorable times of your dance training. Summer Intensives are curriculum-led ballet trainings often taking place at professional ballet companies over a set time period. They require auditions- highly competitive ones, for which you might have to travel to and plan ahead. Whether or not you plan to pursue a professional career in ballet, auditions play a major role in your experience as a ballerina. Summer Intensives can be a great way to experience the daily lives of ballerinas, as you are offered the opportunity to live with other dancers and train in the same studios where real ballerinas take professional class every day. Who wouldn't want to spend a summer learning how to be the best dancer? Check out some of the top programs in the Scholarships & Training Section on page 70.

Sources:
http://greenvilleballet.com/about-ballet/long-term-benefits-of-ballet/
https://www.dosomething.org/us/facts/11-facts-about-arts-education
https://www.arts.gov/sites/default/files/Research-Art-Works-NDEO.pdf

LITTLE MISS DANCEY PANTS BOOK *Series*

LITTLEMISSDANCEYPANTS.COM

ALISON STROMING'S DANCE BAG ESSENTIALS

Being Prepared For the Road Ahead

Professional Division at Dance Theatre of Harlem

School of American Ballet accepted her at only nine years old and through hard work that manifested itself in commuting on the Subway, long hours spent in the studio, and ultimately, breaking new ground in professional ballet, she went on to dance professionally with American Ballet Theatre's Studio Company, Alberta Ballet of Canada, and even a solo performance with Grammy award-winning artist Sarah McLachlan.

Imagine a life filled with alluring photo shoots, hours of dancing your heart out, months of exotic travels, and worldwide admiration. Alison is a professional ballerina, model, designer and spokesperson, who is constantly on the move onstage and off. Currently in her second season with Dance Theatre Harlem, this self-made ballerina-businesswoman has also launched a chic, new leotard collection under Company No.5.

Originally from Recife, Brazil, Alison arrived in the United States through adoption at age four and was raised in New York City. She candidly opens up to fans about a childhood struggle with insecurity and a lack of confidence. Now stunning and successful at 26, her cheerful spirit shines on camera while spilling pirouette tips. She is proof: The sky is the limit once you believe in yourself.

While the life of a ballerina is exciting, no one understands better than Alison how to be prepared for busy the road ahead. Check out her suggestions for must-have items to include in your dance bags.

© Jordynn Buehner

Photo Credit: ©TaKiyah Wallace, Brown Girls Do Ballet | Sweatproof Makeup for dancers by Mymovemakeup.com

No.1 A good firm ball to roll out any sore and tight muscles. Either a tennis ball or lacrosse ball works well.

No.2 A pair of pants to keep your muscles warm when resting. Capezio has great trash bag pants. They are a must
have for dancers.

No.3 Headphones! I always need music while warming up for class or getting ready for performances or photo shoots.

No.4 A notebook. I love to keep one in my bag for taking notes, corrections, thoughts, and sometimes choreography to help me remember.

No.5 Keep a good spray to help balance the shoe odors.

No.6 Snacks andw water, because it is important to keep your body fueled for the day and to stay hydrated. I highly recommend Emergen-C and something with electrolytes to keep you hydrated.

Refreshing foot spritz for dancers | www.freshifyspritz.ca

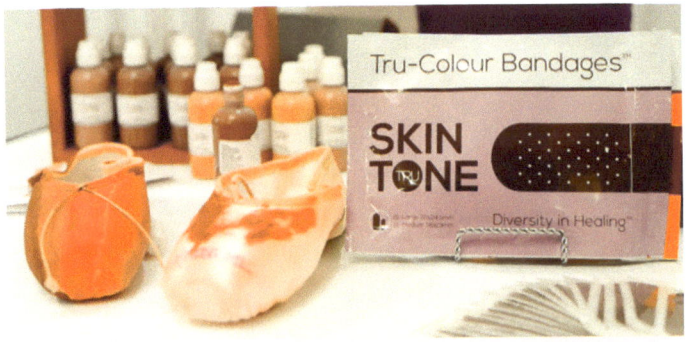

Photo Credit: ©Takiyah Wallace, Brown Girls Do Ballet | Hue Polish by KineticEssentials.com | Flesh Tone Bandaids by Trucolourbandages.com

No.7 You never know when you might need an extra leotard or pair of tights!

No.8 Keep a small kit of any first aid supplies, sewing kits, and hairpins! It is so helpful to have everything you need in one place in your dance bag!

Dancer: Luz Marie Iturbe Ortiz
Photo Credit: ©Justin Reid

A BRAND THAT UNDERSTANDS

"Wearing Gaynor Mindens strengthens your feet. Some people say differently, but for me it has changed my feet completely. I had biscuits, like, really flat feet. And the fact that these are plastic shoes means you really have to articulate your feet; it makes them stronger and just, better."

—Michaela DePrince

Diversity

It's no secret that brown ballerinas face many obstacles on a daily basis, and have struggled to gain acceptance in the classical ballet world. Little did we know, Gaynor Minden shares a similar journey. Skepticism, gratitude, and suspicion are some of the words used to describe the initial reaction to their innovative brand. It's only natural that they understand the need for a customizable shoe that could help every foot shape achieve a photo-worthy arch! We had a chance to speak with them and learn why Gaynor Mindens are a favorite among brown ballerinas.

Straight From the Experts: How to Select Proper Pointe Shoes.

Get fitted. An ill-fitting shoe makes it harder to work properly on pointe—which is hard enough as it is! A properly fitted pointe shoe should hug your foot all over (without squeezing or pinching), and it actually should look like your foot. If you're seeing the shoe more than you're seeing the line of your leg, that's a good indicator it's not a proper fit

Specifically with Gaynor Mindens, it is crucial to select the appropriate shank strength and box shape for your foot type, as they are made out of a flexible polymer that doesn't change shape or soften. (This means no smashing boxes or breaking shanks!) However, these materials are what keep the shoe durable over time, ultimately giving them a longer lifespan. The box shape should be determined by the shape of your toes, (and width of your metatarsal) without a toepad on. The shank strength really depends on the dancer, but ideally, dancers should go as soft as possible. A comfortable shank allows your feet to get stronger while also giving you more control over the shoe. What more could a dancer want?

A Pre-Arched Shank

That's right: Gaynor Minden shoes come pre-pointed. For dancers who may not have a highly-arched foot, a shoe with a little curve can help achieve the proper shape. Gaynor Mindens also have a lower profile than many other pointe shoes, which allows for a more delicate look.

The Gaynor Minden Shoe...

Uses a modern set of materials, making it innovative and durable. Where other brands still use traditional materials—paper, paste, burlap, nails, cardboard, etc.—Gaynor Mindens are made from resilient, durable elastomers lined with shock absorbing material to make them more comfortable, longer lasting, and quieter. There also aren't any pleats at the bottom of the shoes, so they're very stable. Adding to their originality, they were first brand to differentiate between the shape of the box and the width of the shoe. This allows dancers to easily mix and match different specs to customize their shoes. Gaynor Mindens were designed with the intention of making a shoe that actually supports the work that dancers do, rather than just making the work possible.

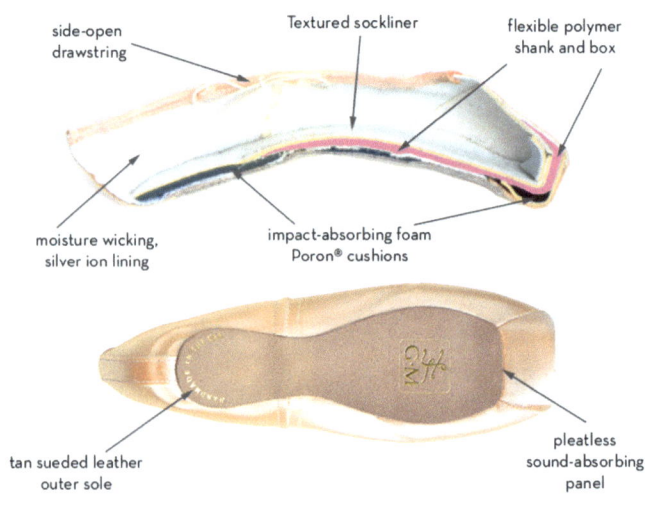

Life Span and Shoe Care

For the financially-savvy momagers, ballerinas have reported that Gaynor Mindens can last 3-5 times longer than a traditional shoe. This, of course, depends on the dancer, but they are designed with materials that last longer. Viengsay Valdés (Principal, National Ballet of Cuba) told the company she once wore one pair of shoes for an entire tour of Swan Lake.

Gaynor Mindens structural components don't absorb water, but simply airing them out helps with odor control. Also, for the prima ballerina who loves a pretty shoe (like us!), Gaynor Mindens can be gently cleaned with delicate soaps like Woolite and a soft wash-cloth.

For more information on Gaynor Mindens, visit their website at: **www.dancer.com**

The Best Methods for Ordering

Gaynor Minden shoe fitters highly recommend being fitted at your local Gaynor Minden retailer. Absolutely nothing replaces being able to try the shoes on in person, under the watchful eyes of an experienced fitter. Fitters are also available via email or phone to answer questions should you need to order online. Their website has a customized shoe option where experts can suggest a size for a dancer based on tracings and photos.

As a dancer, you might often hear talk of shoes being designed for narrow to wide feed but we have confirmed Gaynor Mindens are not created for one particular foot type. With over 4,000 size combinations (including a amazing new Sculpted Fit model) they can fit almost anyone!

AUDITION TIPS

How She Made it Into the Ranks of New York City Ballet

Olivia Boisson
Corps de Ballet at New York City Ballet

By age 13, she had already faced her first serious knee injury and was forced to hang up her tutu for a year, something that would discourage most aspiring ballerinas. However, experiencing life without ballet fueled a determination to heal and dream of someday joining the ranks of New York City Ballet. After years of dedicated training and studying Balanchine, she became the first black woman to dance with NYCB in over a decade after Aesha Ash's departure.

The dance world taught me strength and how not to give up.

-OLIVIA **BOISSON**

This is a much-needed characteristic to survive in the competitive ballet world, especially in auditions, as a dancer's life revolves around preparing for opportunity that could change your life in the time of one ballet class. You would be hard pressed to find a teacher that doesn't allude to George Balanchine's remarkably high standards for the New York City Ballet. With beginnings dating back to 1933, NYCB is considered one of the most prestigious ballet establishments in American history, and is arguably one of the most difficult companies in the world to stake place in. Olivia Boisson made the cut by the time she was 21.

As the daughter of Haitian immigrants, Olivia's culture is largely influenced by French elements, creating a deep appreciation of the arts and languages. Like many young Haitian girls, Olivia was introduced to ballet at the age of seven by her mother, who had also grown up taking various forms of dance. Instructors saw her potential early on, and while she was a bit timid at first, she found power in expressing herself through movement. After four years of training under the legendary Arthur Mitchell, Founder of Dance Theatre of Harlem, Olivia was accepted into the School of American Ballet.

Nearly 12 years later, you can find the NYCB corps member beaming in selfies with artists like Alicia Keys or posing at fashionable galas throughout New York City. Landing a coveted position opened the doors for the experience of a lifetime, filled with culture, art, and of course, hours spent dancing in the legendary Lincoln Center studios. Here's what she had to say about preparing for the big audition day:

No.1 Prepare a clear resume with pictures you feel confident about. Be sure to read all requirements and registration details carefully prior to your arrival.

No.2 Make sure you arrive early and warm up properly. Pack extra everything! Tights, hair pins and water.

No.3 Follow the dress code but wear something you feel comfortable in (including shoes that are already broken in.) Try not to wear something too distracting. You want your presence to be remembered, not your attire.

No.4 Keep your makeup natural and hair well-groomed. Concealer, light foundation, blush and finish with mascara. Simple is better when it comes to auditions.

No.5 Don't compare yourself to the other dancers! Just concentrate on yourself. A lack of confidence shows when dancing. Focus on your strengths!

When the audition is over, don't feel bad if they don't contact you. You can always audition again. There are plenty of other opportunities and companies.

Visit **www.nycballet.com** for tour dates. You can follow Olivia's ballerina life instagram at **@toughinatutu**

Jimena Flores Sanchez
Professional Division, Pacific Northwest Ballet

"From a very young age, I was taught to embrace myself and stay true to my cultural origins. Moving to the United States from Mexico was a challenge in many ways. There were times I was told I was too short or simply not slim enough to succeed in this art form. Today, I accept my differences. Having these dissimilarities encourages determination toward my dreams."

Photo Credit: ©Jade Butler

DANCING

Photo Credit: ©TaKiyah Wallace, Brown Girls Do Ballet | ©Justin Reid | ©Renee Scott
©Pickled Thoughts Photography | ©Jasmine Anderson

POWER IN AUTHENTICITY

The Extraordinary is Possible When You Embrace Your True Self

Ingrid Silva

Professional Division at Dance Theatre of Harlem

If you study the lives of those who influenced future generations, you will be sure to find one common denominator: Originality. Martha Graham, Virginia Johnson, and Alvin Ailey all made incomparable contributions to this world by remaining true to themselves. Authenticity is what inspires change when society tells us differently.

Authenticity is what comes to mind when introduced to ballerinas like Ingrid Silva. The warmhearted, Brazilian-naturalista glows with confidence onstage and in person. Her story is anything but conventional, and further confirms why she's an inspiration to many.

Originally from Rio de Janeiro, Ingrid grew up in the working-class neighborhood of Benfica. She took her first ballet class at eight years old through Dançando Para Não Dançar, a program that provided classical ballet training to children and teens that could not otherwise afford dance classes. The program had a successful track record of dancers moving on to dance professionally with the Teatro Municipal Company, a prominent dance company in Rio de Janeiro. She later had the opportunity to train with the Teatro Municipal School but after realizing there were not any black female dancers in the professional division, Ingrid knew she would have to go abroad for better opportunities. By the time she was 18, she made it to New York City through Dance Theater of Harlem's summer intensive program. A year later, she was offered a position in the company.

She recalls that her assimilation to the United States ballet world was not difficult, since ballet is a universal language. Perhaps Brazil's pressing issues of race also allowed for more optimism, even with the limited number of companies featuring black ballerinas here. It should also be noted that she moved to the United States completely alone and didn't know any English. She had to make it solo, on her own.

Still, she didn't accept pressure from U.S. standards. When asked about her decision to rock her natural tresses, a concern from many brown ballerinas due to the European aesthetics traditionally casted in roles, she states, "I have never felt pressured by any standards. Ballet has it's own beauty within movement and I believe each person possesses their own unique beauty as well."

With few ballerinas she could relate to, Ingrid realized she had to become her own role because she had to make it all alone. Aside from skin color, her reality was quite different than the ballerinas she was exposed to at the time. She recognizes where she comes from, but now realizes the universal impact being a black dancer has throughout the world. She dreams of someday returning to Brazil to help younger girls who are like her.

The 26 year old is now living her dreams, without doubt or conforming to expectations. She is proof that the extraordinary is possible when you embrace all parts of yourself, and discover power in authenticity that allows you to fulfill them.

Follow Ingrid's incredible journey on instagram at @ingridsilva

Visit www.dancetheatreofharlem.com for performance schedules.

Dancer Chelsea Simone
Photo Credit: ©Justin Reid

Dancer: Ebony Williams | Former Dancer with Cedar Lake Contemporary Ballet | Photo Credit: ©Takiyah Wallace, Brown Girls Do Ballet

Ch. 6

THE RECIPE FOR A HEALTHY BODY IMAGE

Avoiding Unhealthy Comparisons

Sydney Magruder

Former Trainee with Conneticut Ballet

Guess Contributor
SYDNEY MAGRUDER

Photo Credit: © Justin Reid

Do you find yourself constantly comparing your-self to the other dancers in your class? Are you always covered in warmups to hide your body? Do you find yourself wishing you had better feet, longer legs, a smaller chest?

Every dancer has been there, wondering whether or not her body is right for the demanding and often narrow-minded world of classical ballet. As time marches on, the aesthetic in ballet has opened, even if only slightly, to welcome dancers with more diverse body types - more muscular, tall and short alike, the list goes on. Even as the ballet world changes little bit by little bit, it can be stressful and painful to compare yourself and your body to your fellow ballerinas. Here are some tips to avoid unhealthy comparison and appreciate yourself!

1. FLAUNT YOUSTRENGTHS:

Go shopping! Find the leotard line that makes you look your best and feel confident. If you look lovely, your dancing will be lovely as well. As a young ballerina, I received a compliment on my neckline from a teacher I greatly admired. Ever since then, I've been partial to v-neck and princess-cut (cinched at the breastbone) leotards that show my collarbone and shoulders. If you have a uniform and aren't permitted to wear the shape that flatters you, don't fear. Try to jazz your hair up with pretty pins for your bun, or pretty stud earrings that make you feel fabulous.

2. LOOK FOR ROLE MODELS:

We're always fawning over the gorgeous ballerinas on Instagram, because let's be honest, aren't they all just #goals? Try to find ballerinas who have bodies similar to your own. You'd be surprised how many beautiful, working classical ballerinas have bodies that don't fit the age-old stereotype. Whether it's large chests, shorter legs or womanly curves, lots of great ladies have made their bodies work for them while totally tackling all of ballet's major roles on stages around the world! Check out powerhouse dancers like Alvin Ailey's Hope Boykin, American Ballet Theatre's Gillian Murphy and Misty Copeland, New York City Ballet's Lauren Lovette, and so many more.

3. TALK TO YOUR TEACHERS:

Try to chat with one of your teachers that you trust about your concerns. More often than not, they will hear your concerns and offer you loving advice or wisdom as to how to manage those feelings and tendencies. It might sound silly to talk to the very person who has a hawk-eye on you every day, but they truly care and will listen to you about how you're feeling. It's pretty likely they'll have gone through this themselves, so don't be afraid to open up and listen carefully.

4. FOCUS ON YOUR UNIQUENESS:

Focus on your uniqueness: Are you a star in petit allegro? Are your extensions darn near perfect? Do you have excellent epaulement? Work it. Focus on your strengths and unique qualities that make you stand out, and learn to love your ballerina self. After all, most people you pass on the street can't do anything we do in a day. Be proud of your hard work as a ballerina and flaunt what makes you special, every single day!

5. EVALUATE YOUR DIET:

Regardless of your body type, being a dancer requires making adjustments to your eating habits. It takes some time to get used to it, but you will feel more energized. My favorite snacks are roasted chickpeas, kale chips, seaweed snacks, and some prepackaged snacks by the Enjoy Life brand - they're safe for my allergies and are full of vitamins. I'll have a smoothie before class, some veggies and hummus between class and rehearsal, and some tuna on crackers for the trip home. Then, I have something hearty for dinner like turkey chili or salmon and veggies. For eating healthy, try to make vegetables and fruit most of your diet!

While it's completely normal to compare yourself to other dancers, don't let it consume you or ruin your day. If you or a friend feels overwhelmed by negative feelings of comparison or poor body image, talk to your parents, your dance teacher or a school counselor about how you're feeling. They can encourage you, give you skills to help cope, and get you medical attention if you need it.

HAPPY DANCING!

MOVE MAKEUP

FOR WOMEN WHO SWEAT

SWEATPROOF, NATURAL MAKEUP, FOR WOMEN ON THE MOVE

MYMOVEMAKEUP.COM

Eliana Vahaʻi Feʻao Dance Major at Mira Costa College

The Tongan Ballerina "When I first started dancing, I never thought I was a pioneer, that I would make history, or become a role model. That's the power of ballet. Tongans are brown-skinned, muscular people. We don't fit the image most people have when they think of ballet. So what? Let's change the image. Let's be so good they can't ignore us.

Photo Credit: ©Arschana Images

Ch.7

A JOURNEY THROUGH ANGUISHED PASSION
FEATURE STORY ON TUNAI DENISE

Principal Dancer with Eleon Dance Theatre

Photo Credit: ©Jasmine Alston

Ballet was not her first love, but after realizing she had talent that lead to the Rock School for Dance, she turned her insecurities about people's negative remarks into incredible passion and art. Having recently performed on Black Girls Rock and growing through rigorous training, she discovered her purpose through an anguished passion.

Only two years ago, Tunaí Denise was called upon to strike graceful poses in a ballet-inspired fashion photo shoot. She had no idea her face would later make history on the cover of the first book for ballerinas of color. She had no idea the photo shoot theme would be relevant to her own story.

Saniyyah Bilal, Creative Director at Curio Styling, likely saw the same qualities that drew us to Tunai's sweet nature. Humble. Gratitude. Two words that describe her distinctive presence. She spoke with unassuming confidence as she prepared to chaine into an amazing developpe. Being a pleasure to work with is equally important as being talented and our favorite ballerinas are both. With that being said, meet our cover girl, Tunaí Denise.

THE BEGINNING

I was introduced to ballet at a summer dance camp when I was only seven years old. Everyone was required to take at least one ballet class. I hated it at first but soon realized I was actually pretty good. Eventually, I began to take more lessons and later auditionedfor the Rock School for Dance Education. I was the only girl accepted from my program.

For me, ballet became an outlet to clear my mind. I came from a pretty rough neighborhood in Philadelphia, and I would have a lot of emotions bottled up with no idea how to let them out. I could never have imagined someone like me becoming a ballerina. Dancers were so disciplined and vigorous, which was the opposite of me at the time. I would let other people's negative comments get in my head and affect my confidence. That was until I discovered the benefits of ballet.

Anguished Passion- an artistic photo series by Curio Styling, follows the tale of a ballerina fighting to overcome the obstacles of her surroundings.

> Dance is the hidden language of the soul, of the body.
>
> BY **MARTHA GRAHAM**

ANGUISH TO PASSION

Although I was very committed, dancing didn't become my passion until I was in high school. I had a love-hate relationship with ballet. In some ways, I was learning this challenging, technical skill but, on the other hand, it was taking time away from my doing regular kid things. I wasn't really sure if I wanted dance to be my profession. I didn't think I was good enough to make a career out of it. I just couldn't see what other people saw in me. Then, one day, I decided to write down all the great qualities I liked about myself. One of them was resiliency; no matter what the task was, I never gave up. This single quality sparked it all. I told myself, if I'm going to commit to something, I need to give it my all.

Heidi Cruz also largely influenced my decision. She was the first black ballerina I ever saw perform and the only black female dancer at Pennsylvania Ballet at the time. I fell in love with her style and beauty. I could tell she worked very hard. Heidi's movements were so elegant, and her demeanor was so graceful. She made everything seem effortless. I could see she loved what she did. That's exactly how I wanted to feel someday.

Ballet refined me and taught me how to stop internalizing things. I developed a different perspective on life and how I was approaching my goals both personally and training-wise. I learned what it means to have the drive and determination it takes to appreciate a challenge. I gained patience with myself during the process.

WHAT YOUNG GIRLS CAN LEARN

Among many values, I would say ballet training instills discipline, hard work, a graceful presence, and openness to culture. These are all essential life skills beneficial whether ballet is chosen as a profession or not. It also encourages high physical fitness and an active lifestyle.

I believe the dance world has shaped me into the strong woman I am today. Ballet has given me the confidence to believe in myself, which has helped me become more adaptable to any circumstance. From the studio to graduating with a Bachelors of Fine Arts, I learned to master my abilities by being a doer and staying focused. Through ballet, I have discovered my purpose...my God given talent.

You can follow Tunai's dance journey on instagram **@tunaidenise** and more artistic photo shots **@CurioStyling.**

Dancer: Jane King
Photo Credit: ©Justin Reid

BEYOND THE BARRE

Dance Education

Alicia Graf Mack
Former Principal Dancer with Alvin Ailey

It seems obvious to attend college following high school graduation, but dancers feel they face a unique decision: Secure a company spot, or attend college and postpone your ballerina dreams. While their classmates spend time filling out college applications, dancers spend hours auditioning in studios, sometimes asking themselves the question: Can you be a dancer AND a college student? Alicia's inspiring struggle to pursue both proves that greatness can be achieved when doing it all.

Standing 6'2 and completely luminous, many presume Alicia Graf Mack has the ideal ballerina body: Long, slender legs and flexibility that dancers dream of. Not to mention, Alicia came from a highly accomplished family who pursued both academic and artistic endeavors. She was well groomed for early success. With reviews in The New York Times, she was known in the dance world by the time she turned 19. Then at 21, an injury nearly ended it all.

> I was a devastated, as I had never considered my life without dance. I am so lucky that I had received a strong education.

SAID **ALICIA**.

It wasn't a straightforward path, but the credentials would later lead to Smithsonian Magazine naming her an American Innovator of the Arts and Sciences in 2007 and her being named a recipient of Columbia University's Medal of Excellence, among several other honors.

HER STORY

I started taking dance classes at 2.5 years old. I have always been passionate about dance. My mom was a model and she used to exercise and practice her poses at home. I would imitate her from the time I could walk. She decided to put me in creative movement classes. At the age of 11, I became much more serious about becoming a professional ballerina and dedicated all my free time to training. I joined Dance Theatre of Harlem at the age of 17.

Both my parents are academically oriented. My mom, in addition to running a successful modeling school, holds a PhD in Social Work and was a professor at Howard University in Washington, DC. I have 3 siblings, and we all understood that we had to receive strong grades to continue our extra-curricular activities. I had excellent teachers who turned me on to learning and academic achievement. I can remember coming home from dance at 9 or 10 o'clock in the evening and staying up past midnight to finish my homework.

Although I maintained high marks in high school, I decided to go straight into the field instead of attending college. Actually, I moved to New York City before the end of my senior year and earned my high school degree through correspondence at Professional Children's School. Several years into my professional career, I developed Ankylosing Spondilitis and had 2 corrective knee surgeries and a reconstruction on my ankle. This was a devastating time for me, as I had never considered my life without dance. I am so lucky that I had received a strong education, and was accepted into Columbia University in New York. I graduated in three years, with a degree and history, and a job offer on Wall Street in JP Morgan's Marketing Department.

But of course, by this time I had healed from my injuries and was dancing again. That summer, I toured Italy with Complexions Contemporary Ballet. Upon returning, I met Carmen de Lavallade in one of our rehearsals, a legendary dancer, actress and choreographer who I admired. She pulled me aside and told me, "Very few people have the talent that you have, and I think you should make a different plan for your life." I knew this meant something. I called JP Morgan and declined the job offer.

I had a fresh start on my dance career and decided to continue my journey that would eventually made up 34 years as a dancer. I returned to Dance Theatre of Harlem and later joined Alvin Ailey in 2004. My arthritis re-appeared and I was forced to take another break and have more corrective surgeries. During this time, I decided to obtain a Masters degree in Nonprofit Management from Washington University in St. Louis. I have developed a deep love for teaching and I am currently working at Webster University and Washington University in St. Louis. Thankfully, my education has afforded me the credentials necessary to teach dance on the collegiate level.

In 2013, I co-founded D(n)A Arts Collective, with my sister Daisha. We host workshops and training camps in New York City for young, aspiring dancers. We teach classes and recruit well-known dancers and choreographers from various genres of dance to teach and speak to the kids. We aim to enrich the lives of young, aspiring dancers by exposing them to high quality classes and workshops. Witnessing that passion ignite in so many young dancers inspires me.

My advice for aspiring dancers is to understand the world of ballet is extremely competitive. If a dancer goes to school with aspirations to become a professional ballerina, I would encourage that student to attend a strong institution for dance and dedicate their education to training their body. I always encouraged my young students to attend college or look at professional training programs. These are great places to not only earn a degree or certificate, but to start creating a professional network.

I am determined to dance for the rest of my life.

For updates on Alicia's dance world, follow her on instagram at @aliciagrafmack.

Visit www.dnaartscollective.com for class schedules.

Dancer Sydney Winston | Photo Credit: ©Ta'Kiyah Wallace, Brown Girls Do Ballet

A MESSAGE TO BROWN BALLERINAS

Misty Copeland
Principal Dancer at American Ballet Theatre

Ch.9

Dear Brown Ballerinas:

I've often spoken about how I wished I'd known more about the rich history of black women in classical ballet as I was on the journey towards becoming a professional. It was well into my career when I started to learn and read about the Raven Wilkinsons, Virginia Johnsons, and Janet Collins. I was thrilled to find that these women had paved a path for black women like me to be able to dance professionally on some of the most prestigious stages in the world.

So it's a particular honor for me to contribute these words to the first annual publication of Brown Girls Do Ballet's book because this begins the present-day documentation and recognition of brown girls all over the world who are making strides and breaking down barriers in classical ballet. With this book as a physical reminder, our contributions will never be forgotten and will hopefully encourage and inspire brown ballerinas for many years to come.

My personal mantra has become "Never let the words and opinions of others define you." But I hope that the words you will read between these pages will help you form a better understanding of what you can contribute to this art form as you grow to become the artist you have always dreamed of. Merde!

Sincerely,

Misty Copeland

Dancer Sherly Beliard | Photo Credit: ©Pickled Thoughts Photography

Scholarship listings for The Ballerina's Little Black Book

SCHOLARSHIP NAME	AMOUNT	DESCRIPTION	WEBSITE
American Harlequin Floors Scholarship	$500-$5,000	In an effort to provide better opportunities for young people pursuing performing arts careers, American Harlequin awards monthly scholarships to support dancers around the country.	www.harlequinfloors.com
Princess Grace Dance Award	$5,000-$25,000	Established by Princess Grace Foundation, scholarships or fellowships are awarded to a promising dance students for tuition toward professional training at a non-profit school in the United States.	www.pgfusa.org
Ballet In The City Misty Copeland Scholarship	$1,000	The Misty Copeland Scholarship was established in 2014 to honor Ms. Copeland by providing opportunities for a dancer of color in the discipline of classical ballet	www.balletinthecity.org
NYCDA Foundation College Scholarship Program	$5000-25,000	The NYCDA Foundation College Scholarship Program is to award multiple 4 year college scholarships to cover the cost of tuition towards performing arts majors.	www.nycdance.com
Eurotard Scholarship	$1,000	The Eurotard Scholarship was created to assist dance students to be able to pay for tuition, travel, competitions, etc.	www.eurotard.com
The Kelvin Coe Scholarship	$1,000	The Kevin Coe scholarships award is intended to enable further studies of classical ballet to talented individuals based on need and prodigy.	www.enavantfoundation.com
Beverly Miller Costume Gallery Dance Scholarship	$500-$1,00	The Beverly Miller scholarship is intended to help young people to pursue their dance education. Costume Gallery awards ten thousand dollars each November for students to put towards their dance education.	www.usascholarships.com
Dance Like Tiffany is Watching Scholarship	$250-$500	The Tiffany Mogenson Memorial Fund awards scholarships to dancers ages 7-21 who wish to pursue additional dance education or dance-related opportunities	www.charitysmith.org
The Renee and F. Howard Walsh, Jr. Scholarship	$5000	This scholarship from Texas Christian University to help support ballet majors.	www.dance.tcu.edu
Brown Girls Do Ballet Annual Summer Intensive Scholarship	$500	The annual Brown Girls Do Ballet Summer Intensive Scholarship is awarded to young dancers ages that have been accepted, have registered for a summer intensive program, and exhibit financial need. This scholarship is intended to cover additional costs associated with dance needs.	www.browngirlsdoballet.com

TRAINING PROGRAMS

Our picks for top ballet training programs based on ballerina reviews and of course, stellar reputation for technique. The following institutions offer summer intensive programs, housing accomodations, and scholarships to assist with covering tuition cost.

SCHOOL OF AMERICAN BALLET (SAB)
www.sab.org

ALVIN AILEY AMERICAN DANCE THEATRE
www.alvinailey.org

AMERICAN BALLET THEATRE
www.abt.org

JOFFREY SCHOOL OF BALLET
www.joffreyballetschool.com

DANCE THEATRE OF HARLEM
www.dancetheatreofharlem.org

HOUSTON BALLET
www.houstonballet.org

DEBBIE ALLEN DANCE ACADEMY
www.debbieallendanceacademy.com

WASHINGTON BALLET
www.washingtonballet.org

THE KIROV ACADEMY
www.kirovacademydc.org

BALLET AUSTIN
www.balletaustin.org

We'd like to thank
the following friends and partners for their support of
The Ballerina's Little Black Book

THE BALLERINA'S
LITTLE BLACK BOOK

1ST EDITION

by Brittani Marie

www.ingramcontent.com/pod-product-compliance
Lightning Source LLC
Chambersburg PA
CBHW041533220426
43662CB00002B/48